DO NOT REMOVE
CARDS FROM POCKET

4-3-87

By
Carolyn Gloeckner

Edited By
Dr. Howard Schroeder
Professor in Reading and Language Arts
Dept. of Elementary Education
Mankato State University

Produced & Designed By

Baker Street Productions, Ltd.

CRESTWOOD HOUSE

Mankato, Minnesota
U.S.A.

LIBRARY OF CONGRESS CATALOGING IN PUBLICATION DATA

Gloeckner, Carolyn.
Marvin Hagler.

SUMMARY: A biography of the middleweight champion chosen Boxer of the Year for 1983 by the World Boxing Council.
1. Hagler, Marvin, 1954-   —Juvenile literature. 2. Boxers (Sports)—United States—Biography—Juvenile literature. [1. Hagler, Marvin, 1954-   2. Boxers (Sports) 3. Afro-Americans—Biography] I. Schroeder, Howard. II. Title.
GV1132.H28G57   1985   796.8'3'0924   [B]   84-12689
ISBN 0-89686-257-7

International Standard Book Number:	Library of Congress Catalog Card Number:
0-89686-257-7	84-12689

PHOTO CREDITS

Cover: Focus on Sports
Wide World Photos: 4, 7, 8, 10, 17, 24-25, 31, 32-33, 34-35
Sports Illustrated: (John Iacono) 13, 19, 37, 44; (Manny Millan) 22, 40-41, 45
United Press: 21, 28, 39, 42-43, 46

Hwy. 66 South, Box 3427
Mankato, MN 56002-3427

TABLE OF CONTENTS

Marvin always wanted to be somebody!

DREAMING BIG

Marvin Hagler wanted to be somebody! He dreamed about being a famous athlete. He often dreamed he was Mickey Mantle or Walt Frazier or Floyd Patterson. It made him feel good.

Marvin Nathaniel Hagler was born on May 23, 1954. His father left the family when Marvin was eleven. His mother, Ida Mae, worked very hard to raise six children. The family lived in a ghetto neighborhood in Newark, New Jersey.

Ida Mae had her hands full, with two sons and four

4

daughters. What worried her most was what went on in the streets. She wanted to protect her children, so she was very strict.

"Mind your own business," she'd say. "Come straight home from school. Stay home until I get home. Stay away from strangers." There were to be no drugs or prisons for her children. She would see to that! She also saw to it that her children had what they needed. She made sure they were properly dressed. Their clothing might not be new, but it was clean. "We took care of what we had," Marvin's sister Veronica remembers.

The oldest Hagler child, Marvin, was a lonely person. He liked animals, though, and often brought home injured birds. He kept pigeons in a coop on the porch. Marvin also kept a turtle on the fire escape. Sometimes he let it swim in the bathtub. Ida Mae was not too happy about that!

When he was ten, Marvin met a social worker named Joe. Joe took him to a park where they flew kites. Joe taught Marvin what he knew about sports. He gave Marvin boxing gloves and showed him how to use them. Marvin's uncles taught him, too.

Ida Mae remembers that Marvin always said he'd be a boxer someday. He wanted to be like Floyd Patterson.

THE NEWARK RIOTS

On July 12, 1967, when Marvin was thirteen, Newark became a battleground. There was a five-day race riot.

Looking down from their third-floor apartment, the Haglers could see the mob. Looters ran in every direction. To Marvin, they looked like ants on a picnic table—like ants with crumbs. They were carrying furniture, TV sets, and appliances.

Ida Mae wouldn't let her children leave the apartment. She double-locked the door and pushed a chair under the knob. For three days, the family stayed there. Once, bullets smashed through the window and into the wall. After that, Ida Mae kept the children away from the windows. They had to crawl from room to room. She wouldn't let anybody stand up.

When the riot ended, twenty-six people had been killed. The streets were littered with garbage. Stores were in ruins.

Then, two years later, it happened again. There was another riot in Newark. There was more looting and more shooting. No one was killed. But Ida Mae had had enough.

MOVING TO BROCKTON

Ida Mae called a relative in Brockton, Massachusetts, and asked for help in finding a place to live. Then she packed up her children and her furniture. The Haglers moved to Brockton.

Life was different in Brockton. For one thing, Ida Mae eased up on her children. She let them go outside, and left

6

*Just as friends did for him, Marvin introduces
young fans to boxing.*

her doors unlocked. Her new neighborhood was much
safer than her old one.

Marvin was used to living in an all-black neighborhood.
Here, there was a mixture of black and white. He had to
learn to trust white people. "When I found out all white
people weren't bad, I started to relax around them," Marvin remembers. "It took me a long time."

Marvin had quit school at fourteen. In Brockton, as in
Newark, it was easy to get into trouble. "I was running a
lot, and stealing a little," he said. What kept him from
serious trouble was boxing and the Petronelli brothers.

Marvin still trains in Brockton, where he first started boxing.

8

Guareno (Goody) and Pascuale (Pat) Petronelli were partners in a construction company. They also owned a gym.

Marvin went there one day when he was fifteen. He hung around and watched. Goody asked him if he wanted to learn to fight.

Marvin said, "Sure, yeah." But he wasn't so sure. The Petronellis were white. He had a hard time accepting their help. But he loved boxing so much that his feelings soon changed. Goody became his trainer and Pat became his manager. That's what they are to this day.

Goody says that Marvin had the desire to be a boxer. "He'd get a swollen lip or a black eye and come back the next day. Those are the kids you look for." Marvin was a left-hander, a "southpaw." He developed a strong, quick punch. He loved boxing, the fancy moves, and the gloves. "I liked the smell of them, the look, the feel, just putting them on, trying to hit someone with them, trying to get out of the way from getting hit..."

Goody told Marvin he was a natural. "He taught me combinations, and I would go home and practice them in front of a mirror," Marvin recalls.

"MARVELOUS" MARVIN

So Marvin went into amateur boxing. He had to lie about his age. He told officials that he was two years older than he really was. It was the only way they would let him box.

Marvin's skill in the ring helped him win fifty out of fifty-two amateur fights. In 1973, at 158 pounds, he won the 165-pound championship in the National Athletic Association Union finals. He gave the trophy to his mother for a Mother's Day gift.

Marvin's style, as a fighter, was shaped when he was an amateur. He had started shaving his head. He thought it

made him look tougher. Marvin also got his nickname "Marvelous" during his amateur years. A writer in Lowell, Massachusetts called him "Marvelous" Marvin after watching him in an amateur bout.

Like Sugar Ray Leonard, Marvin was invited to train for the Olympics, which were coming up in 1976. But by then he was married and had a son. He needed money, not medals.

Sugar Ray Leonard, Leon Spinks, and Howard Davis all went to the Olympics. Their gold medals got them attention. They found it easy to get started in professional boxing. But Marvin passed up the Olympics. In 1973, he had already turned pro. "You can't take a trophy and turn it in for a bagful of groceries," he said.

The truth was, Marvin wasn't sure he would have won any Olympic medals. If he had, it might have helped. It had helped Davis, Leonard, and Spinks.

However, Marvin had trouble breaking into pro boxing. His problem was finding boxers who wanted to fight him.

A SLOW START

Goody decided to also make Marvin a right-hander. He thought it would give Marvin an edge in fights. So Marvin went to work. He used his new style to win his first professional bout. On May 18, 1973, he knocked out Terry Ryan in two rounds.

After that, Marvin could use either hand. Today he switches back and forth as he likes.

Marvin started shaving his head as an amateur so he would look tougher.

Marvin's next two bouts were wins, too. He won the first by a decision. He won the second by a knockout.

In his fourth bout, Marvin finally started making some money. The fight was against a Brockton man named Don Wigfall. Wigfall had beaten up Marvin at a party in 1970. Marvin was glad for a chance to fight him. In eight rounds, Marvin beat Wigfall by a decision and earned $1000.

MOVING TO PHILADELPHIA

And so it went, with win after win. Marvin had seventeen straight wins until November 26, 1974. On that day, he had a repeat match with Sugar Ray Seales. (He had beaten Seales a few months earlier.) The judges called the fight a draw. However, many people felt that Marvin was the clear winner.

But Marvin still couldn't get any big matches, or any big money. He was such a good fighter that nobody wanted to fight him. Marvelous Marvin was too good for his own good!

In 1975, Marvin went up against "Mad Dog" Johnny Baldwin. It was a match he was expected to lose. Promoter Sam Silverman had arranged the fight. He believed that if Marvin clearly lost, he could arrange more matches for

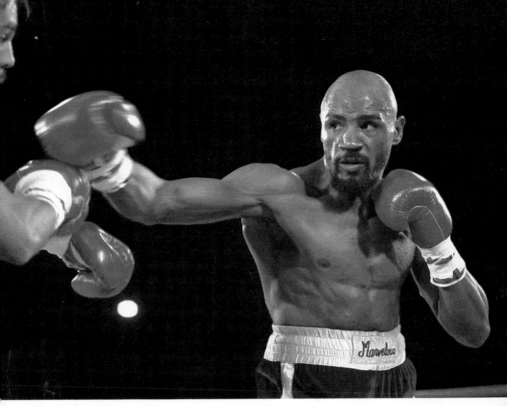

Marvin's ability to throw a strong punch kept him from getting fights early in his career.

Marvin. Boxers wouldn't shy away from a fight with Marvin if they knew that he had lost at least once.

But Marvin beat Baldwin in ten rounds. He earned his biggest purse so far—$2000. But he wasn't happy.

Marvin had been doing construction work for the Petronelli brothers to support his family since 1971. He was good at it, too. He felt that he didn't really need boxing to make a living. But he still had his dream.

The dream went back to the days when Marvin signed his autograph for fans after an amateur fight. He signed it, "Marvin Hagler, future Middleweight Champion of the World." He still wanted to make that dream come true.

But it didn't come easily to Marvin Hagler. He couldn't get the matches. Other boxers wanted to stay away from his powerful jabs. Boxer Joe Frazier once told him, "You have three strikes against you. You're a southpaw. You're black. And you can punch." In Brockton, Massachusetts, that added up to somebody who had trouble getting matches.

So Marvin moved to Philadelphia. Maybe he could get matches in a new town.

LOSING

His first fight was with Bobby "Boogaloo" Watts, on January 13, 1976. He lost in ten rounds. It was a decision loss, though. And plenty of people booed when the decision was announced. It looked to them as if Marvin had won, not Boogaloo.

His fight with Willie "The Worm" Monroe on March 9, ended the same way. It was a ten-round bout, and ended with a decision. The Worm had won. This time, though, there was no doubt. Even Marvin said he had lost. "I still have a few things to learn," he said. "I have a feeling that Willie's already learned them."

Later, he said that the fight with Monroe was a good

thing. It showed him that he would have to train harder if he wanted to be a champion.

Next, Marvin took on "Cyclone" Hart. It was a fight he looked forward to. One day in the gym, Hart was bragging to Marvin. "You're looking at the next Middleweight Champion of the World," he told Marvin. Then Hart slammed his fist into a punching bag.

Marvin, however, stopped him cold during their match. Hart never came out of his corner for the ninth round.

The victory over Hart got Marvin a rematch with "The Worm" on February 15, 1977. This time, the fight ended differently. Marvin landed a right hook in the second round. He followed up with a left hook. Down went "The Worm."

The fight showed how much Marvin had changed in a year. He had more confidence. His punches were quicker and stronger.

Now Marvin got a chance at Bennie Briscoe. It was a strange fight. Both boxers were wearing dark-red trunks. Both were black men with shaved heads. It was hard to tell them apart. But the judges didn't have any trouble. They declared Marvin the winner after ten rounds.

Most fight fans now agreed that Marvelous Marvin was a great fighter. Some of them called him the uncrowned middleweight champion. It began to look to Marvin as if he'd stay uncrowned. He couldn't get a fight with any of the big-name middleweights.

Marvin remembers that Pat and Goody told him he had to keep winning. Before every fight, they said if he won, he was on his way to the big time. But it didn't work out that way. "Every time I won, there was nothing. Every day I was out there running, getting knocked around in the gym, keeping sharp, getting ready for that day."

Marvin got sick of waiting. He wanted to move to California. Maybe his chances would be better there!

The Petronelli brothers argued with him. So did Bertha Walker, a friend. Bertha and Marvin had been friends for years. Both had been married once before. Both had children from their first marriages. Marvin's son was four. Bertha's son was ten and her daughter was eight. Bertha and Marvin were surprised to find themselves growing closer. Soon they became engaged. (They were married on June 21, 1980.)

A CHANCE AT LAST!

The arguments worked. Marvin decided not to go to California. Then, finally, after years of waiting, he got his chance. Vito Antuofermo, the World Middleweight Champion, agreed to fight him.

The two fighters couldn't have been more different. Antuofermo was a brawler. He just lowered his head and started punching. His punches were powerful. Once he got close enough, it was all over. He just punched away until his opponent dropped.

He could take it as well as he could dish it out, too. Antuofermo often left the ring bleeding from many cuts

Marvin prepares for his fight with Antuofermo.

on his face. He'd won forty-five of his forty-nine fights. (One had been a draw.)

Marvin, on the other hand, was a sharp, clean puncher. He liked to stay away from an opponent. He had won forty-six of his forty-nine bouts. Thirty-eight of them he had won by knockouts.

BRAWLING IN LAS VEGAS

The fight with Antuofermo was scheduled for November 30, 1979. It was held in Caesars Palace, in Las Vegas. (The fight was to take place just before the fight between Sugar Ray Leonard and Wilfredo Benitez.)

The Petronelli brothers warned Marvin to stay away from Antuofermo. He must stay away from the corners and off the ropes. Above all, he must not let Antuofermo get close enough to start punching.

Through most of the fight, Hagler was looking good. Antuofermo was soon bleeding from many cuts. That didn't stop the Champion. He hardly seemed to notice his injuries. He kept going after Marvin with everything he had.

Then, in the fourteenth round, Marvin stopped being cool. He went at Vito like a street fighter. He and Antuofermo stood in the middle of the ring swinging away at each other. Fight fans were amazed. They'd never seen such power and strength!

Finally, the fight ended. It had gone the whole fifteen rounds. The referee, Mills Lane, was sure Marvin had won. He said to Hagler, "Now stay facing this way until they announce the decision and I raise your arm." But when the decision came, it was a draw. A draw, in a title fight, means the champion wins.

For Marvin, it was a shock. He felt the decision was unfair. He was sure he had won.

Many people thought that Marvin had beaten Antuofermo.

18

After the bout, former Heavyweight Champion Joe Louis came up to Marvin. He said, "You won that fight. Don't give up."

Marvin said, "I'll be back in the gym tomorrow."

He'd had his shot at the title. Now he knew he could win it. He would keep training and keep on fighting. At least, he had earned $40,000 from the fight. It was his first big money.

Right away, people called for a rematch. Hagler should get a second chance at Antuofermo. But the Champion said no. He didn't want to face those Marvelous punches again right away!

Soon, it didn't matter what Vito Antuofermo wanted. In March of 1980, Alan Minter of England beat Antuofermo. A rematch was set. The World Boxing Association ruled that the winner of the second match had to fight Hagler. Otherwise, the Champion would lose his title. Minter won again.

DODGING BOTTLES IN LONDON

On September 27, 1980, Alan Minter and Marvin Hagler fought for the middleweight title in London, England. Before the fight, there was ugly talk. The newspapers quoted Minter as saying that he wasn't "letting any black man take the title from me." Hagler, the papers said, refused to shake hands with Minter, saying "I don't touch white flesh." The fight was made to seem like a fight between races, not between two men. (Later, both men denied these stories. Marvin said he never shakes hands with someone he is to fight. Minter later stated that he had only said he would not let "that black man" take the championship.)

Minter didn't think much of Hagler before the fight. "He blew his big chance in Vegas, didn't he? He couldn't end Antuofermo." Minter was sure he could beat Hagler.

Marvin had his own ideas about what had happened in Las Vegas. "Know what I did? I softened Antuofermo up. Minter just beat what was left of him."

Marvin lands a right against Alan Minter in London, England.

Minter couldn't lose, in any case. He was going to get $500,000 for the fight. (Hagler would get only a fourth of that.)

Minter was a national hero. The fans that crowded into the arena for the fight were excited. When Marvelous Marvin showed how marvelous he was, they exploded.

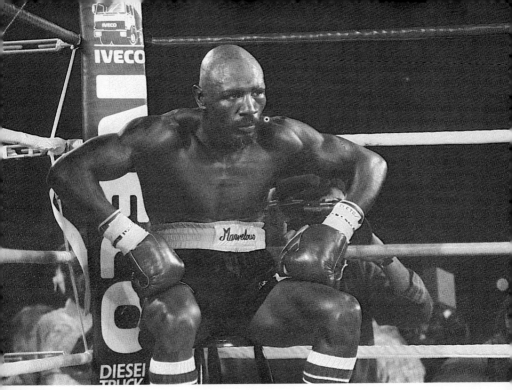

Marvin waits in his corner between rounds.

Minter was taking an awful beating! In round three, with Minter bleeding badly, the fight was stopped. Marvin fell to his knees, his hands raised in victory.

The crowd screamed in fury. They began to throw beer bottles into the ring. The Petronellis came over to protect Hagler with their bodies. British policemen rushed up. They helped the fighter and his handlers out of the ring.

Later, Goody said, "I'd been warned that we'd hear a lot of noise. But I never expected the bottle throwing. Not in England."

Marvin was glad not to have been hurt. But he had another feeling, too. He was disappointed. He had won!

He was the new Middleweight Champion! But there hadn't been time for the referee to raise Marvin's arm in victory. His chance for that moment of glory was gone for good. Instead of glory, there had been angry cries from the crowd.

When Marvin got back to Brockton, a huge crowd was there to cheer him. There was a motorcade from the airport. Fans gathered at City Hall. The mayor gave him the keys to the city.

Marvin said that he'd had a dream about this moment. He dreamed that he came from a "place where there was all hatred to a place where there was nothing but love..."

DEFENDING THE TITLE

Marvelous Marvin was still looking for the big money. He knew that Sugar Ray Leonard had earned twelve million dollars beating Thomas Hearns. Marvin had never even made a million.

Now was Marvelous Marvin Hagler's chance at some rich fights. He was the Champion now. He was the one to beat. Middleweights would have to come to him! Things had changed—a lot. Marvin had to change, too. "I've gotten meaner since I became Champion," he said. "They're all trying to take something from me that I've worked long and hard for. I like the feeling of being champ."

Marvin's first opponent as the Champion was Fulgencio Obelmejias.

UNBEATEN OBELMEJIAS

Early in January, 1981, Hagler was training to fight Fulgencio Obelmejias from Venezuela. His earnings would be half a million dollars for the fight.

Obelmejias had never lost a fight. He had won thirty bouts, twenty-eight by knockouts. But Marvin was not impressed. Obelmejias, he said, had fought only second-rate boxers.

On January 17, Hagler fought the Venezuelan. In eight rounds, he wore the challenger out. He won by a TKO (technical knockout) in the eighth round.

THE ANTUOFERMO REMATCH

Next, Marvin got his chance to take on Vito Antuofermo again. Both boxers hoped for a clear win. To get ready, Antuofermo had had surgery. His problem was the bony ridges over his eyes. They stuck out so far that his skin was easily cut. The blood from his wounds blinded him during a fight.

A doctor smoothed the ridges down. Antuofermo hoped it would make a difference when he fought. Already, he had won a fight after the surgery. He had been cut—but not over the eyes. It looked as if the operation had worked.

As far as Marvelous Marvin was concerned, he had beaten Antuofermo once. He would beat him again, new brow ridges or not.

To train, Marvin went to Provincetown, Massachusetts, on Cape Cod. He had been training there since 1977. He liked running on the beach. He had even named the seagulls he saw on his runs.

Getting away to train was important to Marvin. The only people who came with him were the people who helped him train for a fight. They were all business. Marvelous Marvin needed to be away from the fans. "It gives you a chance to keep your feet on the ground."

In the winter, he ran in the snow. Dressed for the cold, he ran for miles. His trainers and sparring partners were his only company. He liked the quiet. He felt it helped him "get mean" for a fight.

In the spring, Marvin worked out hard, too. Goody Petronelli sparred with him, trying to fight like Antuofermo would. Goody was pleased. The Champion was in fine shape. Goody thought Marvin was sure to beat Antuofermo.

Fight fans were sure Hagler would win the bout. They were right. Thirty seconds into the first round, Hagler was pushing Antuofermo into the ropes with hard punches. Antuofermo moved to get away, and he bumped heads with Hagler. Blood flowed from cuts over the challenger's eyes.

Antuofermo lasted only five rounds. A TKO was called, and the fight was over. Hagler had kept his title.

But Marvin Hagler was bitter. He was still waiting for

Marvin knocked Antuofermo to the canvas in the third round of their fight.

the really big money. He envied Sugar Ray Leonard, who had become famous so fast. He envied the money Sugar Ray had earned.

"I've paid my dues. Now I'm waiting for some big money," he said. For the second Antuofermo fight, Hagler earned $500,000. But it didn't seem like much beside Sugar Ray's millions.

THE MILLION-DOLLAR FIGHT

Mustafo Hamsho was the next challenger Marvin had to beat. He had a record of only one loss in thirty-four fights. "He can't fight a lick," Goody said. But Marvin would have to watch out for butts (hits with the head, which are against the rules in boxing). He would also have to watch out for shots below the belt (also against the rules). But Goody was sure his fighter would win. Marvin was sure, too. This was to be his first million-dollar fight!

Hamsho's manager said his fighter didn't have any style of fighting. "He just wades in, throwing punches from any angle." But Hamsho was tough and brave. He could take a lot of punches without going down.

Marvin knew it wouldn't be easy. It wasn't. The fighters didn't waste any time getting started. In the first round, they were throwing hard punches. Hamsho cut the Champion. Marvin went to his corner bleeding over one eye.

By the third round, both fighters were badly cut. But the fight went on and on. In the tenth round, the referee stopped the fight when Hamsho was in danger of being badly hurt. Marvin had won! He had kept his title.

It took five stitches to close the cut above Marvin's eye. Hamsho had fifty-five stitches!

Hamsho's manager was impressed. He said of Marvin, "I knew he was a great puncher and that he was strong. But I didn't know he was such a beautiful boxer."

STILL EL CAMPEON

Fulgencio Obelmejias wanted a rematch. He felt sure he could beat Marvin Hagler. He explained why he had lost the fight on January 17, 1981. It was the chilly Boston winter. He'd had a cold. "If I hadn't been sick in Boston, things wouldn't have gone the way they did. I would have won and been Champion."

So a rematch was set. This time it would take place during the summer, in Italy. Marvin was glad to defend his title. He had defended it four times so far. He had beaten Obelmejias once. Then he had fought Antuofermo and Hamsho. The fourth match, with Caveman Lee on March 7, 1982, had lasted only sixty-seven seconds. Marvin had knocked the boxer out in the first round.

It was after the Caveman Lee fight that Marvin changed his name. He asked a TV broadcaster to put his name on the screen as Marvelous Marvin Hagler. The broadcaster

Both fighters were careful in the early rounds of their second fight.

30

wouldn't. But Caveman Lee had his name on the screen as Caveman Lee. Marvin was mad, so he went to court. He had his name changed legally, to Marvelous Marvin Hagler.

After winning again and again, Marvin had confidence. But he knew he had a problem, too. He had broken a rib in training on June 22, 1982.

At the weigh-in, Obelmejias angered Marvin. Obelmejias raised his arms above his head as if he had won. He kept saying, *"El campeon, el campeon,"* (the Champion). "I fix Hagler, I fix!"

Marvin did not like that. To him, a fight was a serious matter. Fighting, not talking, would show who was *el campeon*. He called Obelmejias a "punk." He said he would show the challenger who really was the Champion.

In the first few rounds, nothing much happened.

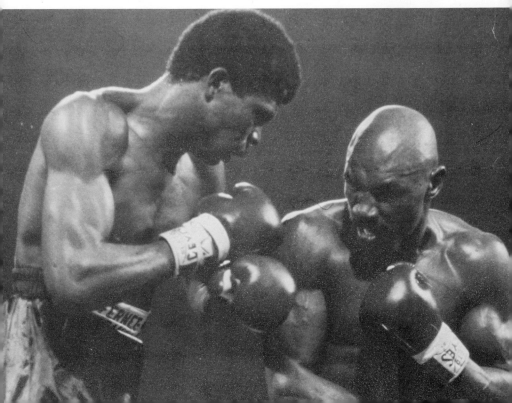

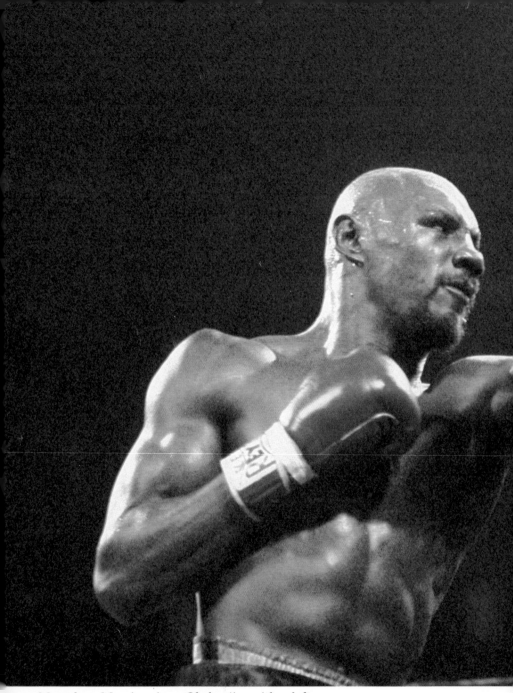

Marvelous Marvin misses Obelmejias with a left.

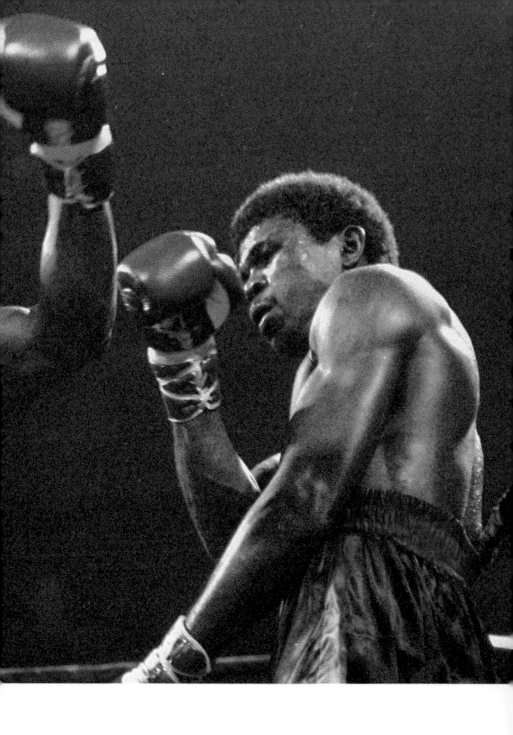

Obelmejias had trained well for the fight. Whenever Marvin got close, he tried a right uppercut. Marvin was careful to stay away from the punch. In the fourth round, Marvin picked up steam. He threw light jabs and punches. In the fifth, he tried a hard right hook. It landed. Obelmejias fell

Marvin was still the Champion!

to the floor. He looked as if he couldn't believe what had happened. He tried to get up, but couldn't.

Pat and Goody agreed that it had been a beautiful punch. Their man had won again. Marvin Hagler still had his title.

He had something else, too. Sugar Ray Leonard was thinking about a fight with Hagler. Leonard was the Welterweight Champion. But he was eager to take on Hagler.

It would mean big money for both of them. At least twenty million dollars for Sugar Ray, and maybe twelve million for Marvin. Fight fans would pay well to see a match like that. TV networks would pay well to broadcast it, too.

An eye injury kept Leonard out of the ring for many months. Finally, his doctors said it was all right for him to go back. But on November 9, 1982, Sugar Ray told fans he had decided to quit. He would never fight again.

Marvin was disappointed. He had looked forward to a great fight—a big money fight.

TWO MORE CHALLENGES

Marvin still had his title to defend, though. In 1983, he would go up against Tony Sibson of England. They fought in Worster, Massachusetts.

Marvin was rough and tough, as usual. He battered Sibson with left-handed punches. He switched to his right hand now and then, just to confuse Sibson.

"I couldn't find him for the first two rounds," Sibson said. "I figured I'd find him sooner or later, but I never did." He said he knew Marvin was there somewhere. After all, he kept getting hit!

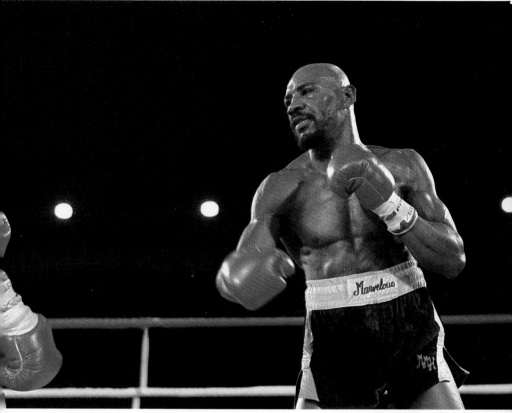

Marvin can punch well with both lefts and rights.

In the fifth round, Sibson was cut over his left eye. In the next round, he went down. Hagler had hit him with a left, than a right hook, then another left. Sibson got to his feet. After a standing eight count, Hagler knocked Sibson down again. This time it was final. Sibson was bleeding badly. He got to his feet, but the referee ended the fight.

"I never believed anyone could do to me what he did," Sibson said after the fight. Sibson had never been cut before. But it took seventeen stitches to close the cuts made by Hagler. Sibson said he had looked at himself in the mirror. "I didn't know fighters could look like this," he said. "That Hagler is an artist in there!"

Next, Marvin took on Roberto Duran. Duran was a tough fighter. He had held the lightweight and welterweight titles during his career. He had lost the welterweight title to Sugar Ray Leonard in 1980. He had returned to fighting as a junior middleweight (not over 154 pounds). Comeback bouts showed he was still a great fighter. He had knocked out Ken Buchanan in June, 1983, to win the junior middleweight WBA (World Boxing Association) title.

Now he wanted a chance at Marvin.

By the time of the Duran fight, November 10, 1983, Marvin had defended his title seven times. He had won all the fights by knockouts. His last fight, on June 3, had been with Wilford Scypion. It had been no match at all. Marvin had knocked Scypion down in the beginning of the fourth round.

Duran, on the other hand, was a skilled fighter. And he really wanted to win this bout. He intended to last the whole fifteen rounds.

Marvin knew what he was up against. He wasn't going to get close enough for a real pounding. In the opening rounds, both fighters were "fighting smart." Neither went

*Roberto Duran and Marvin met before their
fight for a photo session.*

Duran was a skilled fighter who wanted to win.

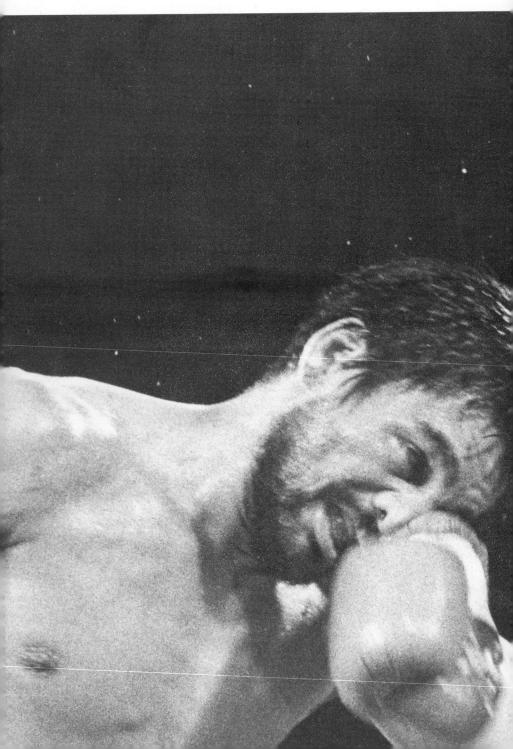

Roberto gets a right from Marvelous Marvin.

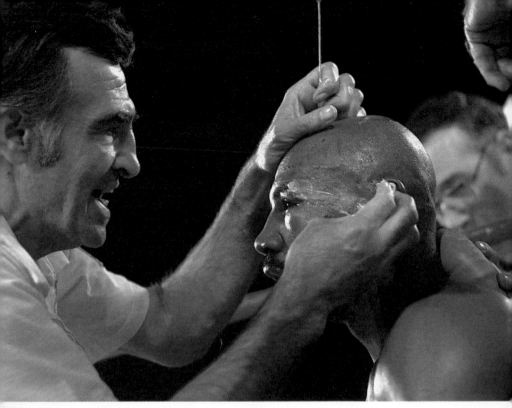

Marvin gets a cut fixed between rounds.

on the attack. Both waited, trying to get a feel for the other boxer's style.

Things warmed up during the fourth round. Hagler began switching from his left to his right-handed stance. Hagler began to wear down his opponent. By the eighth round, Duran was returning fewer and fewer of Hagler's punches.

Duran came back a little in the ninth. He was getting in some hard punches. Now it was Marvin's turn to dodge. He was trying to stay out of Duran's way! To fans, it seemed the fighters were just dancing around.

The judges found it a hard fight to call. But after fifteen

Marvin and his fans celebrate his victory.

rounds, Hagler was declared the winner. He was still the Middleweight Champion.

A GREAT MIDDLEWEIGHT

Marvelous Marvin was finally somebody! People were saying he was one of the great middleweights of all time. He seemed to get better with every fight. He had never been knocked out. He fought a cool, smart fight. His punches were hard, fast, and right on target.

The World Boxing Council picked Marvin Hagler as

"I've got to be the best!"

Boxer of the Year of 1983. Marvelous Marvin said that his title was "worth all the long years and the lonely miles."

To Marvin Hagler, fighting is an art. It's an art he's always learning more about. It's an art he's always getting better at.

"After you reach a goal, you want to keep on growing," Marvin says. "I love fighting. I always say you have to enjoy it like a boy, but play it like a man." About his career in the ring, he says, "I have nothing else. This is all I've got. I've got to be the best!"

Many people think he's already reached that goal. They say Marvelous Marvin Hagler is the best!

MARVELOUS MARVIN HAGLER'S PROFESSIONAL STATISTICS

W = Won   L = Lost   D = Draw

1973

May 18—Terry Ryan	W
July 25—Sonny Williams	W
Aug. 8—Muhammad Smith	W
Oct. 6—Don Wigfall	W
Oct. 26—Cove Green	W
Nov. 18—Cocoa Kid	W
Dec. 7—Manny Freitas	W
Dec. 18—James Redford	W

1974

Feb. 5—Bob Harrington	W
Apr. 5—Tracy Morrison	W
May 4—Jim Redford	W
May 30—Curtis Phillips	W
July 16—Robert Williams	W
Aug. 13—Peachy Davis	W
Aug. 30—Ray Seales	W
Oct. 29—Morris Jordan	W
Nov. 16—George Green	W
Nov. 26—Ray Seales	D
Dec. 20—D. C. Walker	W

1975

Feb. 15—Don Wigfall	W
Mar. 31—Joey Blair	W
Apr. 14—Jimmy Owens	W
May 24—Jimmy Owens	W
Aug. 7—Jesse Bender	W
Sept. 30—Lamont Lovelady	W
Dec. 20—Johnny Baldwin	W

1976

Jan. 13—Bobby Watts	D
Feb. 7—Matt Donovan	W
Mar. 9—Willie Monroe	D
June 2—Bob Smith	W
Aug. 3—D. C. Walker	W
Sept. 14—Eugene Hart	W
Dec. 21—George Davis	W

1977

Feb. 15—Willie Monroe	W
Mar. 16—Reginald Ford	W
June 10—Roy Jones	W
Aug. 23—Willie Monroe	W
Sept. 24—Ray Phillips	W
Oct. 15—Jim Henry	W
Nov. 26—Mike Colbert	W

1978

Mar. 4—Kevin Finnegan	W
Apr. 7—Doug Demmings	W
May 13—Kevin Finnegan	W
Aug. 24—Bennie Briscoe	W
Nov. 11—Willie Warren	W

1979

Feb. 3—Ray Seales	W
Mar. 12—Bob Patterson	W
May 26—Jaime Thomas	W
June 30—Norberto Cabrera	W
Nov. 30—Vito Antuofermo	D
(For World Middleweight Title)	

1980

Feb. 16—Loucif Hamani	W
Apr. 19—Bobby Watts	W
May 17—Marcos Geraldo	W
Sept. 27—Alan Minter	W
(Won World Middleweight Title)	

1981

Jan. 17—Fulgencia Obelmejias	W
June 20—Vito Antuofermo	W
Oct. 3—Mustafa Hamsho	W

1982

Mar. 7—Caveman Lee	W
Oct. 30—Fulgencio Obelmejias	W

1983

Feb. 18—Tony Sibson	W
June 3—Wilford Scypion	W
Nov. 10—Roberto Duran	W

1984

Mar. 30—Juan Holdan	W